# REALLY EASY JAZZIN' ABOUT
## fun pieces for
## PIANO/KEYBOARD

GW00658147

## CONTENTS

# PAM WEDGWOOD

**FABER ff MUSIC**

# Track 1

*You can use a funky drum beat with this one.*

Pam Wedgwood

# PING-PONG

*You can try a dixieland beat to this piece.*

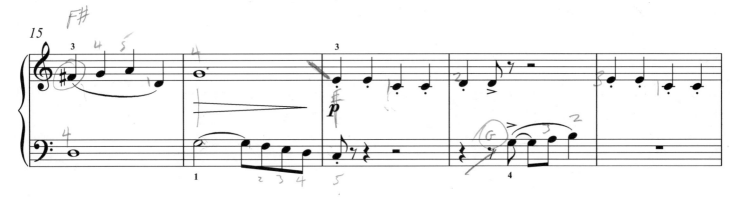

*for Clementine*

# In the eyes of a tiger

*You can try a disco drum beat with this piece.*

# DUAL CONTROL

*You can use a medium rock beat with this piece.*

# Hot Chilli

*You can use a samba rhythm with this piece.*

# Hip-hop

*You can use an 8-beat pop rhythm with this piece.*

# Garage Sale

*You can use a heavy rock rhythm with this piece.*

# WISE GUY

*You can use a jazz waltz rhythm with this piece.*

# Night Patrol

*You can use a medium 8-beat rhythm with this piece.*

# Popcorn

*You can use a relaxed swing rhythm with this piece.*

# Your First Hit Single

*You can use a rock 'n' roll beat with this piece.*

# Big Chief Little Foot

*A chance for you to use the pedal on the right.*

# Moonlight Shadows

*You can use a slow ballad accompaniment with this piece.*

*for Stuart*

# The Jumping Bean

*You can try a disco beat with this piece.*

# Jammy Dodger

*You can use a ragtime rhythm with this piece.*

# Washing-up Blues

*You can use a slow swing beat with this piece.*

# The Swinging Sisters

*You can use a swing beat with this piece.*

# A sad little tale

*You can use a slow waltz beat with this piece.*

# Spell it out to me, Baby!

*You can use a swing rhythm with this piece.*

# The JAZZIN' ABOUT Series

PAM WEDGWOOD

Christmas Jazzin' About. Piano                  ISBN 0-571-51507-X

Christmas Jazzin' About. Piano Duet        ISBN 0-571-51584-3

Christmas Jazzin' About. Violin                ISBN 0-571-51694-7

Christmas Jazzin' About. Cello                 ISBN 0-571-51695-5

Christmas Jazzin' About. Flute                 ISBN 0-571-51586-X

Christmas Jazzin' About. Clarinet              ISBN 0-571-51585-1

Christmas Jazzin' About. Alto Saxophone    ISBN 0-571-51587-8

Christmas Jazzin' About. Trumpet             ISBN 0-571-51696-3

Easy Jazzin' About. Piano                     ISBN 0-571-51337-9

Easy Jazzin' About. Piano Duets             ISBN 0-571-51661-0

Green Jazzin' About. Piano                    ISBN 0-571-51645-9

Jazzin' About. Piano                           ISBN 0-571-51105-8

Jazzin' About. Piano Duets                   ISBN 0-571-51662-9

Jazzin' About. Violin                         ISBN 0-571-51315-8

Jazzin' About. Cello                          ISBN 0-571-51316-6

Jazzin' About. Flute                          ISBN 0-571-51275-5

Jazzin' About. Clarinet                     ISBN 0-571-51273-9

Jazzin' About. Alto Saxophone          ISBN 0-571-51054-X

Jazzin' About. Trumpet                    ISBN 0-571-51039-6

Jazzin' About. Trombone                  ISBN 0-571-51053-1

Jazzin' About Styles. Piano                 ISBN 0-571-51718-8

More Jazzin' About. Piano                   ISBN 0-571-51437-5

Really Easy Jazzin' About. Piano           ISBN 0-571-52089-8

FABER ff MUSIC

© 2001 by Faber Music Ltd
First published in 2001 by Faber Music Ltd
3 Queen Square London WC1N 3AU
Cover by velladesign
Music processed by MusicSet 2000
Printed in England by Caligraving Ltd

ISBN 0-571-52089-8